Religious Science

By

ERNEST S. HOLMES

Dean of

The Institute of Religious Science

Los Angeles

Martino Publishing
Mansfield Centre, CT
2010

Martino Publishing
P.O. Box 373,
Mansfield Centre, CT 06250 USA

www.martinopublishing.com

ISBN 1-57898-969-8

© *2010 Martino Publishing*

Cover design by T. Matarazzo

Printed in the United States of America On 100% Acid-Free Paper

Religious Science

By

ERNEST S. HOLMES

Dean of

The Institute of Religious Science

Los Angeles

The CRAFTWAY PRESS

Publishers   Los Angeles

v

Religious Science

Printed in the United States of America

VI

CONTENTS

VII

FOREWORD

ᕙ

RELIGIOUS SCIENCE is the science of
Spirit, a culmination of the age-long search
for Truth. Those responsible for this
movement lay no claim to any special dispensa-
tion of Providence, or a special revelation of
Truth. Religious Science contains the best
thought of the ages and presents this thought
in a manner that can be understood by all.

In presenting these necessarily brief and in-
complete statements the writer does not claim
to have discovered any new Truth. The Truth
has been known by a few in every age, but the
great mass of people has never dreamed that
actually we live in a spiritual world. Today,
however, there is a great inquiry into the deeper
meaning of life because the race has reached a
state of unfoldment where a broader scope is
possible.

To suppose that the Creative Intelligence of
the Universe would create man in bondage and
leave him bound would be to dishonor the Creative Power which we call God. To suppose that
God could make man as an individual, without
leaving him to discover himself, would be to
suppose an impossibility. Individuality must be
spontaneous and can never be automatic. The
seed of freedom must be planted in the inner-
most of man's being. But, like the Prodigal Son

of old, man must make the great discovery for himself.

We see abundance in the Universe. We cannot count the grains of sand on a single beach. The earth contains untold riches and the very air is vibrant with power. Why, then, is man weak, poor and afraid? Religious Science answers these questions. The Divine Plan is one of freedom; bondage is not God-ordained. Freedom is the birthright of every living soul. All instinctively feel this. The Truth points to freedom under Law. Thus the inherent nature of man is forever seeking to express itself in terms of freedom. We will do well to listen to this Inner Voice, for it tells us of a life wonderful in its scope, of a love beyond our fondest dreams, of a freedom the soul craves.

But the great Love of the Universe must be One with the great law of Its Own Being, and we must approach Love through the law. This, then, is the teaching—Love and Law. As the love of God is perfect, so the law of God also is perfect.

We must understand both.

"He that hath ears to hear, let him hear."

The Author.

Religious Science

THE THING ITSELF

CHAPTER I

HATEVER the nature of any principle may be, in so far as it is understood by anyone, it may be understood by everyone who takes the time to investigate it. This does not require an unusual degree of intelligence, but rather, a practical application of what we now know it to be, in order that we may increase our knowledge of it. The study of Religious Science is a study of First Cause, Spirit, Mind, or the Truth, that invisible Essence, that ultimate Stuff and Intelligence from which everything comes—the Power back of creation—the Thing Itself.

ABSTRACT PHILOSOPHY IS NOT NECESSARY

WE SHALL not attempt to go into its abstract philosophy, for this is not necessary. We accept this "Thing"

and believe in It. What we desire is to
know more about It and how to use It.
From proof alone we know we are dealing with a definite principle. If one,
through the conscious use of his knowledge, can produce a certain result he must
know with what he is dealing.

¶ We may speculate upon the abstract
essence of things, upon the nature of God
and what comes first, what is the absolute and what the relative, but — the
united intelligence of the human race
could not produce a grasshopper.

¶ It may seem as though, in dealing with
metaphysics, we are dealing with something that is too abstract. But what is
tangible other than results? Principles
are forever hidden from our eyes. We
accept the deductions of science in so far
as they are proved, and we recognize that
they are built upon immutable, but invisible principles.

THE UNIVERSE NEVER
PLAYS FAVORITES

WE ARE so used to the thought that if we mix colors we get certain other colors, that we do not realize we are dealing with a principle. We know that whoever blends colors will get the same result, but we do not know why; the wisest man living does not know why. We do not have to stretch our credulity any more in metaphysics.

¶ We think of metaphysics, perhaps, as something that only the most profound thinkers have known anything about, but we should remember that we also are thinkers. The profound thought of all ages has stood in awe of Life itself, realizing that here is a power and potentiality, the highest possibilities of which the human intellect cannot fathom.

¶ Universal principles are no respecters of persons, the universe has no favorites and plays none. Therefore, it is written:

[3]

"And let him that is athirst come. And
whosoever will, let him take the water of
life freely" (Rev. 22:17).

NOTHING SUPERNATURAL ABOUT THE STUDY OF LIFE

LET US then approach the Science of
Mind, the Science of Spiritual Psy-
chology, with awe but not with fear, with
truly a humble thought but not with a
sense that we are unworthy. Let us
approach it normally, happily, willing to
accept, glad to experiment, hoping and
believing that as a result of our efforts
we shall each derive a great good, a sound
understanding of the natural laws of Life
as they apply to the individual and his
relationship to the whole universal
scheme of things. This is the simple
meaning of true metaphysical teaching,
the study of Life and the nature of the
law, governed and directed by thought;
always conscious that we live in a spiritual universe; that God is in, through,

around and for us. There is nothing supernatural about the study of Life from the metaphysical viewpoint. That which today seems to us supernatural, after it is thoroughly understood, will be found spontaneously natural.

¶ We all know that many have been healed of physical diseases through prayer. Let us analyze this. Why are some healed through prayer while others are not? Can we believe that there is a God who picks out some man and says, "I will honor your prayer, but I do not think so much of Mr. So and So?" It is superstitious to believe that God will answer the prayer of one above another. Jesus said that God "maketh His sun to rise on the evil and on the good, and sendeth rain on the just and on the un-just" (Matt. 5:45). Since some people have been healed through prayer while others have not, the answer is not that God has responded to some and not to others, but that some have responded to

God more than others. The answer to prayer is in the prayer. But what is a prayer? A prayer is a movement of thought within the mind of one praying, along a definite line of meditation.

¶ What is the mind? No man living knows. We know a great deal about the mind, but not what it is. By mind we mean consciousness. We are now using it. We cannot locate mind in the body, for, while the body is a necessary vehicle for consciousness here, it is not consciousness. We cannot isolate mind. All we know about it is not what it is but what it does and the greatest philosopher who ever lived knows no more than this, except that he may tell us more of how it works.

THERE ARE NOT TWO MINDS BUT ONLY TWO NAMES

MIND, the Thing, Spirit, Causation is beyond, and yet not beyond, our grasp. Beyond in that It is so big; within, in that, wherever we grasp at It we are It to the extent that we grasp It—but —since It is Infinite we can never encompass It. We shall never encompass God and yet we shall always be in God and of God.

¶ Mind comes under two classifications. There are not two minds but rather two names employed in describing states of consciousness, the objective or conscious and the subjective or unconscious. We think of the conscious state as our conscious use of mind. The subconscious or subjective state of mind, sometimes called the unconscious state, is that part of mind which is set in motion as a creative thing by the conscious state. On page 93 of "The Science of Mind," the text book of The Institute of Religious Science, it is said: "In the Subjective Mind of man we find a law obeying his word, the servant of his Spirit. Suggestion has proved that the subconscious mind acts upon our thoughts without question or doubt. It is the mental law of our Being and the creative factor within us. It is unnecessary, at this point, to go into all the details of the Subjective Mind and its mode of action; it is enough to say that within us is a mental law, working out the will and purposes of our conscious thoughts. This can be no other than OUR INDIVIDUAL USE OF THAT GREATER SUBJECTIVE MIND WHICH IS THE SEAT OF ALL LAW AND ACTION, AND IS 'THE SERVANT OF THE ETERNAL SPIRIT THROUGH ALL THE AGES'."

LIMITLESS POWER
AT MAN'S DISPOSAL

MARVELOUS as the concept may be it is none the less true that man has at his disposal, in what he calls his subjective mind, a power that seems to be Limitless. This is because he is One with the Whole, on the subjective side of Life. ¶ Man's thought, falling into his subjective mind, merges with the Universal

Subjective Mind and becomes the law of THE THING his life, through the one great law of all ITSELF Life.

¶ There are not two subjective minds. There is but one subjective mind; and what we call our subjective mind is really only the use that we are making of the One Law.

¶ Each individual maintains his identity in Law through his personal use of It; and each is drawing from Life what he thinks into It.

¶ To learn how to think is to learn how to live, for our thoughts go into a Medium that is Infinite in Its ability to do and to be.

¶ Man, by thinking, can bring into his experience whatsoever he desires, if he thinks correctly and becomes a living embodiment of his thoughts. This is not done by holding thoughts but by knowing the Truth.

¶ Within us, then, there is a creative field that we call the subjective mind;

around us there is a creative field that we call subjective; one is universal, the other is individual, but in reality they are one. There is one mental law in the universe and where we use it, it becomes our law because we have individualized it. It is impossible to plumb the depths of the individual mind because the individual mind is not really individual but is individualized; behind the individual point is the universal which has no limits. In this concept alone lies the possibility of eternal and endless expansion. Everyone is universal on the subjective side of life and individual only at the point of conscious perception. The riddle is solved and we all use the creative power of the Universal Mind every time we use our own mind.

ALL THOUGHT IS CREATIVE

SINCE this is true it follows that we cannot say that some thought is creative while another is not. We must say that all thought is creative, according to the nature, impulse, emotion or convic- tion behind the thought. Thought creates a mold in the subjective in which the idea is accepted and poured and sets power in motion according to the thought. Ignorance of this excuses no one from its effects, for we are dealing with law and not whimsical fancy.

¶ The conscious mind is superior to the subjective and consciously may use it. Great as the subconscious is, its tendency is set in motion by the conscious thought and in this possibility lies the path to freedom. The Karmic Law is not Kismet. It is not fate but cause and effect. It is a taskmaster to the unwise; a servant to the wise.

ROAD TO FREEDOM LIES NOT THROUGH MYSTERIES

EXPERIENCE has taught us that the subjective tendency of this intelligent law of creative force may consciously be directed and definitely used. This is the greatest discovery of all times. There is no mystery here but a profound fact and a demonstrable one. The road to freedom lies, not through mysteries or occult performances, but through the intelligent use of nature's forces and laws. The law of Mind is a natural law in the spiritual world.

¶ But what do we mean by the spiritual world? We mean the world of conscious intelligence. The subjective is a world of law and of mechanical order; in our lives it is largely a reaction, an effect, a way. It is never a person although it often appears to act as though it were one. Right here many are completely misled, mistaking subjective impulses for actual personalities. This, however, is a field of investigation not fully to be considered here.

¶ The simplest way to state the proposition is to say that we have a conscious mind that operates within a subjective field that is creative. The conscious mind is Spirit, the subjective mind is law. One is a complement of the other and no real individuality could be expressed without a combination of both.

¶ No man has ever plumbed the depths of either the conscious or the subjective life. In both directions we reach out to Infinity and since we cannot encompass Infinity we shall always be expanding and always enlarging our capacity to know and to experience.

¶ We need not ask why these things are so. There can be no reason given as to why the truth is true. We do not create laws and principles but discover and make use of them. Let us accept this position relative to the laws of Mind and Spirit and see what we can do with them rather than how we may contradict the inevitable. Our mind and spirit is our echo of the "Eternal Thing" Itself, and the sooner we discover this fact the sooner we shall be made free and happy. The universe is filled with Spirit and filled with law. One reacts to the other. We are Spirit and we are law. The law of our life reacts to our spiritual or material concepts and builds and rebuilds according to our beliefs and faith.

LEARNING TO TRUST WILL MAKE US HAPPY

THERE is a power in the universe that honors our faith in it; there is a law in the universe that exacts the "uttermost farthing."

¶ We are torn by confusion, by conflict, by affirmation and denial, by emotion, congested by fear, congealed by pride. We are afraid of the universe in which we live, suspicious of people around us, afraid of the salvation of our own souls. All these things negatively react and cause physical disorders.

¶ When we learn to trust the universe, we shall be happy, prosperous and well. We must learn to come under that Divine government, and accept the fact that nature's table is ever filled. Never was there a Cosmic famine. "The finite alone has wrought and suffered, the Infinite lies stretched in smiling repose." God is always God. No matter what our emotional storm or what our objective situation may be, there is always a something hidden in the inner capacity of our being that never has been violated. We may stumble, but always there is that Eternal Voice forever whispering within our ear, that thing which causes the eternal quest, that thing which forever sings and sings.

DIVINE NATURE IS IN EVERY MAN

THIS is The Thing Itself. Briefly let us recapitulate. There is that within every individual which partakes of the nature of the universal wholeness and in so far as it operates, is God; that is the meaning of the world Emmanuel, the meaning of the word Christ. There is that within us which partakes of the nature of the Divine Being, and since it

[15]

partakes of the nature of the Divine Being, we are divine. It reacts to us according to our belief in It and it is an immutable law, subject to being used by the
least among us; no respecter of persons,
it cannot be bound. Our soul will never
change or violate its own nature; all the
denying of it will never change it; all the
affirming of it will never make it any
more than it is. But, since it is what it is
and works in the way that it works, it
comes to each of us through his belief.
It is done unto each one of us as we
believe.

¶ We will say, then, that in spirit man
is One with God. But what of the great
Law of the Universe? If we are really
One with the Whole, we must be One
with the Law of the Whole, as well as
One with the Spirit of the Whole.

¶ If we try to find something difficult to
grasp, then we shall never grasp it, because we shall always think of It as being
incomprehensible.

¶ The mind which we discover within us is the Mind which governs everything. This is The Thing Itself and we should recognize its simplicity.

THE THING
I T S E L F

CHAPTER II

RELIGIOUS SCIENCE is not the special revelation of any individual; it is, rather, the culmination of all revelations. We take the good wherever we find it, making it our own in so far as we understand it. The realization that good is universal and that as much good as any individual is able to incorporate in his life is his to use, is what constitutes the Science of Mind and Spirit.

¶ We have discussed the nature of the Thing as being Universal Energy, Mind, Intelligence, Spirit, finding conscious and individualized centers of expression through us, and that man's intelligence is this Universal Mind functioning at the level of man's concept of it. This is the essence of the whole teaching.

UNIVERSAL MIND, OR SPIRIT, IS GOD

THERE is a Universal Mind, Spirit, Intelligence that is the origin of everything; it is First Cause. It is God. This

Universal Life and Energy finds an outlet in and through all that is energized and through everything that lives. There is One Life back of everything that lives. There is One Energy back of all that is energized. This energy is in everything. There is One Spirit back of all expression. That is the meaning of that mystical saying: "In Him we live, and move, and have our being" (Acts 17:28).

¶ The life which we live is the Universal Life expressing through us, else how could we live. Our thought and emotion is the use we make, consciously or unconsciously, of this original creative Thing that is the cause of everything. Therefore, we shall say that the mind, spirit and intelligence which we find in ourselves, is as much of this original creative God as we understand. That this is not robbing God is a self-evident fact. Since we are, then we are real and actual and have existence, and since we can reduce all that is to a fundamental unit, we find that we have this proposition: there is

Spirit — or this Invisible Cause — and nothing, out of which all things are to be made. Now Spirit plus nothing leaves nothing, but Spirit. Hence there is One Original Cause and nothing, out of which we are made. We are made from this Thing. This is why we are called the "son of God."

¶ We now know that this is what we are, because we could not be anything else; but we do not know how much of this we are. When we see It as It is then, we shall see ourselves as we are. We can only see It by looking at It through our own eyes. Hence, we shall find a better God when we shall have arrived at a higher standard for man. If God is to interpret Himself to man, He must interpret Himself through man. And the Spirit can make no gift that we do not accept.

SEED OF PERFECTION
IS HIDDEN WITHIN

THIS Original Life is Infinite. It is good. It is filled with peace. It is of the essence of purity. It is the ultimate of

intelligence. It is power. It is Law. It is THE WAY IT WORKS
Life. It is in us. In that inner sanctuary
of our own nature, hidden, perhaps, from
objective gaze, "nestles the seed, perfection."

¶ In our ignorance of the truth we have
misused the highest power we possess.
And so great is this power, so complete
is our freedom in it, so absolute the do-
main of law through it, that the misuse
of this power has brought upon us the
very conditions from which we suffer.
We are bound because we are first free;
the power which appears to bind us is the
only power in the universe which can
free us. This is why Jesus summed up
His whole philosophy in this simple
statement: "It is done unto you as you
believe." It took a genius to say, "It is
done unto you as you believe." The great
Teacher looked so deeply into nature that
she revealed her fundamental simplicity
to Him. That "believe" and that "as"
symbolize heaven and hell. And so we

suffer, not because suffering is imposed upon us, but because we are ignorant of our true nature.

WORK IS DONE FOR US BY WORKING THROUGH US

THE THING, then, works for us by working through us, and in us, always; and It cannot work for us in any other way. It spreads Itself over the whole universe and shouts at us from every angle, but It can become power to us only when we recognize It as power.

¶ We cannot recognize that It is, while we are believing that It is not. Hence, it is written: "they . . . entered not in because of unbelief" (Heb. 4:6). We may enter in because of our belief, but we cannot enter while there is unbelief. Here we come to a house divided against itself. If we say we can only experience a little good, then we shall experience but a little good. But, if we say, with Emerson, "There is no great and no small to the

soul that maketh all," then we may ex-perience a greater good because we have THE WAY IT WORKS
conceived it.

¶ Therefore, our belief sets the limit to our demonstration of a Principle which, of Itself, is without limit. It is ready to fill everything, because it is Infinite. So, it is not a question of Its willingness, nor of Its ability, it is entirely a question of our own receptivity.

HOW MUCH CAN WE BELIEVE?

WE MUST go the way of the law. This is a fundamental tenet of Religious Science, because nature obeys us as we first obey it, and our obedience to it is our acceptance of it. How much can we believe? As much as we can believe will be done unto us.

¶ When the consciousness speaks, the law receives and executes. When a farmer plants a seed he invokes the law; that which follows is done by the mechanical side of nature which has no volition of its own. Involution is the cause and evolution is the effect. When a practitioner thinks, or gives a treatment, or makes a prayer, he is dealing with involution, the first step of the creative order. This is what the Bible calls the Word; that which follows is evolution, or the unfolding of the word or concept into objective existence.

¶ We are thinking, willing, knowing, conscious centers of Life. We are surrounded by, immersed in, and there is flowing through us, a creative Something, call it what you will. The sum total of all our thought, will, purpose and belief, creates a tendency in this law, that causes it to react to us according to the sum total of that belief.

¶ Ignorance of the law excuses no one from its effects. If, then, certain specific ways of thought and belief have produced limitations, other beliefs will change them. We must treat to believe. The approach should be direct, it should be specific.

¶ Suppose one is laboring under the idea of limitation. His whole thought is a picture of limitation. Where is he placing himself in Mind? Is he saying, "I cannot have and enjoy good things." And he is demonstrating that he cannot have, or accomplish good. It may take time to reshape the basis of his thought; he must commence by saying, "I perceive that because I am what I am—because of this Infinite Thing that over-shadows eternity and finds its abiding place in me, I know that good is now mine—the all good." There is no mental coercion in this; we do not will things to be done; things are brought into being, not by will, but by the power of the self-assertive Truth.

¶ How much can one demonstrate? Just what one can believe. How much can we see, how much can we accept, how much can we find in our consciousness that is no longer repudiated by our own denials? That much we can have.

HAVE CONCEPT OF GOOD
NOT GOOD AND EVIL

THE gardener goes forth in faith to sow his seeds. He has learned that as he sows so shall he reap; that the law works for all alike. We must accustom ourselves to the concept of the impersonalness of the law, the availability of the law and the mechanical accuracy of the law. If we can conceive only a little good that is as much as we can experience. We must instill into the mind the fundamental proposition that good is without bounds: Only good and loving-kindness shall "follow me all the days of my life" (Ps. 23). We must get this concept rather than too much linking of the good and evil. We experience good and evil because we perceive a presence of duality rather than unity.

¶ Then, knowing that The Thing can work for us only through us, let us begin to accept, today, more good than we experienced yesterday and to know we shall reap a harvest of fulfilled desires. The time must come when we shall have left the apparent evil behind, when, in the category of our minds, it shall be rolled up like a scroll and numbered with the things which were once thought to be. ¶ Let us realize and work with this sound knowledge and perfect faith; that, as high as we shall make our mark in Mind and Spirit, so high, shall be Its outward manifestation in our material world.

CHAPTER III

WE SHOULD approach the study of Religious Science rationally, never expecting to derive any benefits from it that its Principle does not contain. For while it is true that we are immersed in an Infinite Intelligence, a Mind that knows all things, it is also true that this Intelligence can acquaint us with Its ideas only as we are able and willing to receive them. The Divine Mind is Infinite. It contains all knowledge and wisdom, but, before It can reveal Its secrets It must have an outlet. This outlet we shall be compelled to supply through our own receptive mentalities.

¶ All invention, art, literature, government, law and wisdom that have come to the race have been given to it through those who have deeply penetrated the secrets of nature and the mind of God.

¶ Perhaps the simplest way to state the proposition is to say that we are surrounded by a Mind or Intelligence that knows everything; that the potential knowledge of all things exists in this Mind; that the abstract essence of beauty, truth and wisdom co-exist in the Mind of the Universe; that we also exist in It and may draw from It. But what we draw from It we must draw through the channel of our own minds. A unity must be established and a conscious connection must be made before we can derive the benefits which the greater Mind is willing to reveal or impart to us.

¶ The Spirit can give us only what we can take; It imparts of Itself only as we partake of Its nature. It can tell us only what we can understand. The Infinite Knowingness becomes our wisdom only in such degree as we embody Its Intelligence. It has been said that we can know God only in so far as we can become God. This is a far-reaching thought and should be carefully scrutinized. It is to be taken figuratively and not too literally, for we cannot really become God, but we can and do partake of the Divine Nature, and the Universal does personify Itself through man in varying degrees, according to man's receptivity to It.

THE UNIVERSE IMPERSONAL

THE universe is impersonal. It gives alike to all. It is no respecter of persons. It values each alike. Its nature is to impart, ours to receive. When we stand in the light we cast a shadow across the pathway of our own experience. Emerson told us to get our bloated carcasses out of the way of the divine circuits.

A RIDDLE OF SIMPLICITY

IT IS a beautiful and true thought to realize that every man stands in the shadow of A MIGHTY MIND, A PURE INTELLIGENCE AND A DIVINE GIVINGNESS. Not alone unto the great comes the soft tread of the unseen guest. The arrogant have not perceived the simplicity of faith, but the pure in heart see God. The farmer has seen the Heavenly

Host in his fields. The child has frolicked with Him at play. The mother has clasped Him to her breast and the fond lover has seen Him in the eyes of his beloved. We look too far away for Reality.

¶ The intelligence by and through which we perceive that there is a Spiritual Presence and an Infinite Mind in the universe, constitutes receptivity to It and decides Its flow through us. We have made a riddle out of simplicity, therefore we have not read the sermons written in stones, nor interpreted the light of love running through life.

¶ To return to a sane simplicity is one of the first and most important things to do. All men receive some light, and this light is always the same light. There is one nature diffused throughout all nature; one God incarnated in all people.

¶ The Divine Incarnation is inherent in our nature. We are immersed in an Infinite Knowingness. The question is how

much of this Reality are we going to express in our own lives? The direct approach is always the best and the most
effective. In so far as any man has spoken
the truth he has proclaimed God, it mat-
ters not what his particular approach may
have been. The scientist and the philosopher, the priest and the professor, the
humanitarian and the empire builder, all
have caught some gleam of the eternal
glory and each has spoken in his own
tongue, that language which is, of itself,
universal.

¶ Let us do away with a ponderosity of
thought and approach the thing simply
and quietly. It is the nature of the universe to give us what we are able to take.
It cannot give us more. If it has given
more we have not yet been able to receive
the greater gift.

¶ There is a teaching that says that God
manifests through everything and is incarnated in all men; that all is Divinity
and that nature herself is the body of

God. The mechanical laws of nature are set and immutable, but the spontaneous recognition of these laws, gives us the power to bring them into practical use in everyday life and experience.

¶ Here we have a dual unity; law and order, spontaneous choice, volition, conscious action, and automatic reaction. The laws of the universe are to be trusted but we must come to understand them before we can use them. Once understood any law is available and is impersonally responsive to each and all alike.

LOVE RULES TROUGH LAW

IN AN intelligent study of the teachings of Religious Science we come to understand that all is Love and yet all is Law. Love rules through Law. Love is the Divine Givingness; Law is the Way. Love is spontaneous; Law is impersonal. We should study the nature of reality with this in mind and in this way we shall avoid two grave mistakes: either viewing life as made up only of mechanical laws, or viewing it as made up only of spontaneous actions, irrespective of law and order.

¶ As we gain the broader viewpoint we shall see that Life must contain two fundamental characteristics. We shall see that there is an Infinite Spirit operating through an Infinite and Immutable Law. In this, Cosmos and not chaos finds an eternal existence in reality. Love points the way and Law makes the way possible.

THE SCIENTIFIC METHOD

IF WE observe any scientific discovery we shall see that this is the way it works. Some man's mind discovers the law or principle governing the science; this is the way of love, of personal volition, of choice. This is the spontaneous element in the universe. Following this knowledge of the way the principle works, having discovered the operation of the law, the spontaneous element now rests its case on immutable reactions in- herent in the law. All science is based upon proven principles.

¶ But we should not overlook the significant fact that it is the MIND which discovers and makes use of the mechanical law. Is not this mind the Spirit in us? But we never completely can fathom the Infinite Mind, we shall always be discovering new lands; consequently evolution is an eternal unfoldment of the more yet to be.

¶ Since it is the mind which must first come to see, know and understand, and since all future possibility for the race must find first an avenue of outlet through someone's mind, we shall do well to look to the mind for the answer to all of our problems.

¶ Undoubtedly we are surrounded by and immersed in a perfect Life, a complete, normal, happy, sane, harmonious and peaceful existence. But only as much of this Life as we embody will really be-

come ours to use. As much of this Life
as we understand and embody will react
as immutable law—the reaction of the
mechanical to the volitional. The concept is wonderful and fraught with tre-
mendous significance. In it is bound up
our hopes and fears, our expectations and
our future and present realizations.

¶ Since an understanding of any law
must pass first through our conscious
mind before we can make use of it, it
follows that with all of our getting we
should get understanding. Should we
wish to know a certain truth, we should
state that this truth is already known in
Mind and this statement will be true, but
the Over-Mind must be accepted into our
mind before we can understand it. How,
then, are we to accomplish the desired
result? By stating and feeling that our
mind knows the truth about the thing
which we desire to know. In this way we
draw the Infinite Mind into our mentalities for definite knowledge of some particular good.

THE Universal Mind contains all knowledge. It is the potential ultimate of all things. To It all things are possible. To us as much is possible as we can conceive, according to law. Should all the wisdom of the universe be poured over us, we should yet receive only that which we are ready to understand. This is why some draw one type of knowledge and some another and all from the same source—the source of all knowledge. The scientist discovers the principles of his science, the artist embodies the spirit of his art, the saint draws Christ into his being, all because they have courted the particular presence of some definite concept. Each state of consciousness taps the same source but has a different receptivity. Each receives what he asks for, according to his ability to embody. In this way the Universal is Infinite; the possibility of differentiating is limitless.

¶ Life always becomes to us the particular thing we need when we believe that It becomes to us that particular thing. The understanding of this is the essence of simplicity. As all numbers proceed from the fundamental unit, as all material forms are but different manifestations of one formless stuff, so all things proceed from that which is neither person, place nor thing, but is of the essence of all things.

¶ Our thought and conscious receptivity differentiate this Universal Possibility by drawing it through our minds and causing it to flow into particular channels through the conscious receptivity of our different faiths. One state of consciousness will differentiate one kind of a result, another mental state a different manifestation.

MENTAL WORK DEFINITE

MENTAL work is definite. Each state of thought taps the same Principle, each uses the same law, is inspired by the same Spirit, but each draws forth a dif-

ferent result. Here is multiplicity pro-
ceeding from Unity. This is what Emerson meant when he said that Unity passes into variety.

¶ But, someone will ask, can we bring out both good and evil from the One Source? Of course not. The First Principle is goodness, and only in so far as our thought and action tends toward a constructive program will it eventually succeed. We cannot fight the universe. It refuses to be budged from its course. We can only go with it. But there is plenty of latitude for personal expression. How, then, are we to know what is right and what is wrong? We are not GOING to know, we already do know. Every man knows right from wrong, in its broadest sense.

¶ It should be considered right to live and to enjoy living. To be well, happy, and to express freedom is to be in accord with Divine law and wisdom. Here is

latitude enough for the most expectant
and the most enthusiastic devotee of
Religious Science.

THE PRINCIPLE RESTATED

LET US restate the Principle of Religious Science. We are surrounded by an
Infinite possibility. It is goodness, Life,
law and reason. In expressing Itself
through us It becomes more fully conscious of Its own being. Therefore, It
wishes to express through us. As It
passes into our being It automatically becomes the law of our lives. It can pass
into expression through us only as we
consciously allow It to do so. Therefore
we should have faith in It and Its desires
and ability to do all for us that we shall
ever need to have done. Since It must
pass through our consciousness to operate
for us, we must be conscious that It is
doing so.

¶ The one who wishes to demonstrate
some particular good must become con-

scious of this particular good if he wishes to experience it, therefore, he must make his mind receptive to it and he must do this consciously. There is no hocus-pocus in a mental treatment. It is always definite, conscious, concrete and explicit. We are dealing with Intelligence and should deal with it intelligently.

¶ There is no occult trick in giving scientific treatments. It is just the reverse. Simplicity should mark our every effort and positivity should acompany all statements that we make into the law of Good.

THE SECRET ALREADY KNOWN

A TREATMENT is a statement into the Law, embodying the concrete idea of our desires accompanied by an unqualified faith in a Law that we now understand works for us, as we work with It. Let us waste no further time looking for the secret of success or the key to happiness. Already the door is open and whosoever will may enter.

¶ Undoubtedly each of us is now demonstrating his concept of life, but trained
thought is far more powerful than un-
trained and the one who gives conscious
power to his thought should be more
careful what he thinks than the one who
does not. The more power one gives to
his thought, the more completely he be-
lieves that his thought has power, the
more power will it have.

TREATMENT ACTIVE, NOT PASSIVE

A TREATMENT is an active thing.
When one gives a treatment he is not
sitting around, hoping that something
may happen; he is definitely, constructively, actively stating, sensing, knowing
some specific good. This is in accord with
the Principle which we seek to demonstrate. If we give treatments without a
definite motive in mind, the most we can
accomplish will be to promote a salutary
atmosphere; a passive meditation will

never produce an active demonstration, any more than an artist can paint a picture by sitting down with his paints without using them. The mind must conceive before the Creative Energy can produce, we must supply the avenue through which It can work. It is ready and willing; it is Its nature to spring into being through our thought and action.

¶ In an iron foundry the pig iron is thrown into a great furnace and melted. That which was solid becomes liquid, and is then poured in molds that are fashioned in different shapes. The iron itself neither knows nor cares what particular form it takes; it was formless, ready to take any form supplied; if we did not place it in the proper molds the liquid would assume no particular form. This is the way it is in dealing with the subtle energy of Spirit, but the molds are made in our own subjective minds through conscious and specific thought, purpose and direction. We should be very careful, not

to think that because we make the mold
we must create the substance. It already
exists, it is part of the Life in which we
live, a part of the Universal Energy.
Definite molds or concepts decide the
shape which is to be created from the
general liquid. This should prove to us
that there is a specific technique in mental treatment that we should not overlook. If we wish a certain good we must
instill into our own minds a realization
of this specific good and then, as this idea
is the mold we place in mind, it will be
filled by the substance necessary for its
complete manifestation of this good in
our lives.

¶ Therefore, if a man is seeking to demonstrate he must tell himself that he has
faith in his power, in his ability, in the
Principle and in the certainty of the demonstration for which he hopes. Faith, being a mental attitude is according to law,
and even though one doubts he can over-
come his doubt and create the desired

faith, definitely. If this were not so, only those who by nature have faith in God could ever hope to understand the Principle of the Science of Mind and Spirit which is subject to certain, definite, immutable and impersonal laws. However, even though faith is a necessary attitude, it is something that can always be established by explaining the theory and proving the Principle.

NO MYSTERY IN TRUTH

𝔉AITH in a certain specific statement has power consciously to oppose, neutralize, erase and obliterate the opposite mental attitude. It is because of this fact that this study is a science that can be definitely used and we must accept it as such. The mystery with which most people surround the search for Truth, relative to this Principle is not read out of It, but is read into It.

¶ It stands to reason that if thought and faith, prayer, hope and appreciation are anything at all, they are definite. And if

[45]

they are definite, then they must be specific, if they are specific then they unques-
tionably must accomplish their desire.

HOPE A SUBTLE ILLUSION

MANY people correctly begin their
treatment in this manner: "I know
that the Principle of Intelligence within
me will direct me, etc.," but then they
complete it with the thought: "Well, I
certainly hope it does." This is entirely
forgetting any definite statement and is
simply wondering if possibly some good
will come along. This is not a correct
treatment, and is not the scientific use of
this Principle. Hope is good, it is better
than despair, but it is a subtle illusion and
is an unconscious compromise having no
part in an effective mental treatment. We
should say to doubt, "Where did you
come from, who is your father, etc. . . .
You have no place in my mind. Get out!
I know that the faith within me now neu-
tralizes ALL doubt." This is the scientific
use of a mental statement. There must
be no compromise with the consciousness.

¶ We have discovered what the Principle is and how It works, now this is
WHAT IT DOES. Specifically turn to
that thought which tells us we do not
know how to use It and repudiate the
falsehood.

¶ The Principle that we have to demonstrate is perfect, and, in so far as we can
compel the mind to perceive this perfection, so far it will automatically demonstrate. Experience has proved this to be
true.

¶ We waste much time in arguing over
things that cannot be answered. When
we have arrived at the ultimate, THAT
IS THE ULTIMATE; it is the way the
thing works. Therefore we have a right
to say that there is a law involved, that
this law executes the word. We discover
laws, find out how they work and then
begin to use them. Therefore this question is answered when we say it is the
nature of thought and of the Creative
Energy, and the nature of Being TO BE

THIS WAY. We would say that Law is an attribute of God. God did not make Law; It co-exists with the Eternal. The Infinite Law and the Infinite Intelligence are but two sides of the Infinite Unity; one balances the other and they are the great personal and impersonal principles in the universe. Evolution is the out-working of the mechanical and involution is the in-working of the conscious and the volitional.

NO LIMIT TO THOUGHT

WHEN we think, something happens to the thought. The field through which thought operates is Infinite. There is no reason to doubt it. No matter how it is approached, to thought there can be no limit and so we will say it is the nature of Being to react in this way. Here and now we are surrounded by and immersed in an Infinite Good. How much of this Infinite Good is our good. ALL OF IT. And how much of It may we have to use? AS MUCH OF IT AS WE CAN EMBODY.

CHAPTER IV

ONE OF THE great difficulties in the new order of thought is that we are likely to indulge in too much theory and too little real practice. As a matter of fact we only know as much as we can prove by actual demonstration. That which we cannot prove may or may not be true, but that which we can prove certainly must be and is, the truth.

¶ Of course the theory of any scientific principle goes beyond its application at any given stage of the unfoldment of that principle, and the evolution of its accomplishments. If this were not true there would be no progress in any science. The sciences are objectively real to us only in so far as we demonstrate them, and until demonstrated they are suppositional so far as practical results are concerned. If there is any field of research where the practical application is necessary, it is in the metaphysical field, the reason being that the Principle of metaphysics seems

[49]

less tangible to the average person than does the principle of other sciences. As a matter of fact all principles are as intangible, but the world at large has not yet come to consider the Principle of mental practice in the same light that it considers other given principles of life and action. Its apparent intangibility is lessened whenever and wherever anyone actually demonstrates the supremacy of spiritual thought force over apparent material resistance.

¶ It is easy enough to rush about shouting that there are no sick people, but this will never heal those who appear to be sick. It is easy to proclaim that there are no needy—anyone can say this whether he be wise or otherwise, and the ones who make such statements are generally otherwise. If we are to prove such statements to be facts in our experience we shall be compelled to do more than announce a principle, no matter how true it may be.

¶ There is no doubt about the immutability and the availability of the law. The Law in Infinite. It is right where we happen to be at any given time. It occupies all space and fills every form with differentiations of Itself. The law also flows through us because It flows through everything, and since we exist It must be in and through us. What It does for us It must do through us. This is the crux of the whole matter. Infinite and immutable as the law is, ever present and available as It must be—the potential possibility of all human probability—It must flow through us in order to manifest for us.

¶ It has been proved that by thinking correctly and by a conscious mental use of the law of Mind, we can cause It to do definite things for us, through us. By conscious thinking we give conscious direction to It, and It consciously or unconsciously responds to our advance along the line of our conscious or subjective direction.

¶ It must and will respond to everyone because It is law and law is no respecter of persons. It will respond to everyone according to his belief in It, and according to his mental and spiritual equivalent of the life of the man and of the Spirit. We are surrounded by an intelligent force and substance, from which all things come—the ultimate essence, in the invisible and subjective world, of all visible and objective forms and conditions. It is around us in Its original state, ready and willing to take form through the impulse of our creative belief. It is Its nature to respond to our belief; It works for us by flowing through us. This law we did not create; this law we cannot change. We can use It correctly only as we understand and use It according to Its nature.

¶ Hence, it follows, that if we believe that It will not work, It really works by appearing to "not work." When we believe that It cannot and will not, then, according to principle It does not. But when It does not, It still does—only It does according to our belief that It will not. This is our own punishment through the law of cause and effect; we do not enter in because of our doubts and fears; it is not a punishment imposed upon us by the spirit of God, but an automatic result of failing constructively to use the law of God.

¶ God does not punish the mathematician who fails to obtain the right answer to his problem. The thought of the unsolved problem does punish him until he applies the right principle and thus secures the desired result. Thus sin and punishment, righteousness and salvation, are logical reactions of the universe to the life of the individual.

¶ When we are dealing with real Life, with thoughts, impulses, emotions, etc., we are dealing with causation, with original Cause and we should be most careful how we deal with such powers and forces. In dealing with this subtle power of Mind and Spirit we are dealing with a fluent force. It is forever taking form and forever deserting the form which it has taken. Thus a practitioner of Religious Science should not be confused over any given form but should know that any form which is not of the original harmony is subject to change. The Original Spirit is harmony. It is beauty and truth and everything that goes with Ultimate Reality. The universe is not divided against itself.

¶ We should learn to control our thought processes and bring them into line with Reality. Thought should tend more and more toward an affirmative attitude of mind that is positive, stable and above all else, toward a real unity with Spirit that already is complete and perfect.

¶ We should be able to look a discordant fact in the face and deny its reality since we know its seeming reality is borrowed from illusion, from chaos and old night.

Our standard is one of perfection. "Be ye therefore perfect, even as your Father which is in heaven is perfect" (Matt. 5:48). We should be able to look at a wrong condition with the knowledge that we can change it. The realization that we have this ability must be gained by the application of our knowledge of Religious Science.

¶ The practice of Religious Science calls for a positive understanding of the Spirit of Truth, a willingness to let this inner Spirit guide us, with the conscious knowledge that: "The law of the Lord is perfect" (Ps. 19:7), and we must believe this to be a fact. In so far as our thought is in accord with this perfect law it will accomplish and nothing can hinder it. "Heaven and earth shall pass away, but my words shall not pass away" (Matt. 24:35), said the beautiful Jesus as he strove to teach his disciples the immutability of the law of righteousness.

¶ A practitioner uses thought definitely and for specific purposes and the more definitely he uses the law the more directly will it respond to him. A false fact is neither person, place nor thing to the one who uncovers it, and once uncovered it has no place to hide. The illusion seen and understood is made negative in the experience of the one who suffered by it. While it is true that wrong conditions exist they could not remain unless there were someone to experience them, consequently the experience must be in consciousness. Change the consciousness and the false condition will disappear. Conditions are not entities. We are entities. Cannot that which is conscious cast out that which has no consciousness? If we properly understood we would be able to remove false conditions as easily as Jesus did. He knew, but our faith is weak. We must strengthen it, and we can.

¶ Let us analyze this: One finds himself impoverished. He wishes to change this condition. He knows that it is not in accord with ultimate reality; that the

Spirit imposes no limitations. Therefore, he knows that his condition has no real law to support it, is simply an experience of consciousness. He wishes a definite result in an opposite direction. First he realizes that the law of Life is a law of liberty, of freedom. He now states that this law of liberty is flowing through him and into all of his affairs. But the image of his limitation persists. Here is a definite contradiction of his statements of freedom. Right here he must stop and declare that these images of limitation are neither person, place nor thing; have no power, personality nor presence and no real law to support them. He does not believe in them and they cannot operate through him. He is free from their influence forever. He then begins to fill his thought with the idea of faith, and the expectancy of good, the realization of plenty. He senses and mentally sees right action in his life. He puts his whole trust in the law of Good and It becomes very real to him as he definitely speaks it into being, into his being and into the being of his affairs. He denies anything and everything that contradicts his realization of this truth.

¶ At this point of realization he meets a friend who immediately begins a tale of woe about hard times, bad business conditions, etc., and should he listen to this "tale of the serpent" he might reverse his previous affirmations and make negative his former mental and spiritual concept. This does not mean that he should refuse to hold conversation with people for fear they will neutralize the position that he has taken in mind, but that he should refuse mentally to accept the false position. Then he can talk with anyone and not be disturbed.

¶ The time will come when we will let our "conversation be in Heaven" and shall refuse to talk about, read or think about those things that ought not to be. But, someone will say, "should we refuse to look at sickness, poverty and unhappi-

ness?" This is not what we are discuss-
ing. We will not refuse to help the help-
less or to lift up the fallen, but we will
refuse to wallow in the mud because of
our sympathies. "And if the blind lead
the blind, both shall fall into the ditch"
(Matt. 15:14).

¶ Of all the people in the world the ones
who have come the nearest to touching
the seamless garment of Truth have been
the most sympathetic and the greatest
lovers of the race. Jesus said, "And I, if
I be lifted up, . . ." (not dragged down)
"will draw all men unto me" (John 12:32).

¶ We are in the world and of it and it is
good that it is so; the world is all right
when we view it correctly. Who knows
what would transpire if all men would
speak the truth. It has never yet been
tried, but let not the mouth of the pro-
fane hinder those who would enter, from
entering. The world has never yet fol-
lowed the simple ethics of Jesus, yet it is
loud in its proclamation that it is Chris-

tion. This statement is not written in a spirit of controversy, it is one of conviction and will make its appeal only to those who are convinced. "A man convinced against his will is of the same opinion still."

¶ Let us return to the man who really wishes to demonstrate the supremacy of spiritual thought force over apparent material resistance. Let us put his treatment in the first person,—impersonating him for the purpose of clarity.

¶ "I am a center in the Divine Mind, a point of God-conscious life, truth and action. My affairs are divinely guided and guarded into right action, into correct results. Everything I do, say or think is stimulated by the truth. There is power in this word that I speak because it is of the Truth and it is the Truth. There is perfect and continuous right action in my life and in my affairs. All belief in wrong action is dispelled and made negative. Right action alone has power and right action is power and power is God, the

living Spirit Almighty; this Spirit ani-
mates everything that I do, say or think.
Ideas come to me daily and these ideas
are divine ideas. They direct me and sus-
tain me without effort. I am continuously
directed. I am compelled to do the right
thing at the right time, to say the right
word at the right time, to follow the right
course at all times. All suggestion of
age, poverty, limitation or unhappiness is
uprooted from my mind and cannot gain
entrance to my thought. I am happy,
well, and filled with perfect Life. I live in
the Spirit of Truth and am conscious that
the Spirit of Truth lives in me. My word
is the law unto its own manifestation and
will bring to me or cause me to be brought
to its fulfillment. There is no unbelief,
no doubt, no uncertainty. I know and I
know that I know. Let every thought of
doubt vanish from my mind that I may
know the truth and that the truth may
make me free."

¶ The Truth is instantaneous in its demonstration, taking only such time in its

unfoldment as is inherent in the law of a logical and sequential evolution. In this invisible law of unfoldment we must come to trust, and although we do not see the way we must believe that the way is and is operative. We must trust the invisible, for it is the sole cause of that which is visible; ". . . things which are seen were not made of things which do appear." (Heb. 11:3).

¶ Healing and demonstration take place as our minds become attuned to the truth of Being. There is no process of healing, but there generally is a process in healing. This process is the time and effort which we undergo in our realizations of Truth.

¶ The one who wishes scientifically to work out his problems must daily take the time to meditate and mentally treat the condition no matter what the apparent contradictions may be. He is working silently in the Law and the Law will find an outlet through his faith in It.

¶ This law is the law which puts the act into all action. It is the invisible actor working through us to will and to do. As a result of right treatment the mold formed in the subjective mind by the treatment makes possible a concrete manifestation. The treatment is an intelligent energy in the invisible world. It is a spiritual entity working through the law of Mind and it is an actual force now consciously directed. Therefore it must produce specific results.

¶ This will not seem strange to those who have given thought to the subject. As the primordial Word of the Creator is the only thing which explains creation, so every man's word, partaking of this original nature must reproduce the creative function in his life at the level of his consciousness of the One Life back of, in and through all.

¶ A treatment is a spiritual entity in the mental world and it is equipped with power and volition,—(as much power and

volition as there is faith in it, given to it
by the mind of the one using it) and,
operating through the law, it knows ex-
actly how to work and what methods to
use and just how to use them. We do not
put the power into this word but we do
let the power of the law flow through it
and the one who the most completely be-
lieves in this power will produce the best
results. This is the law of cause and
effect again.

¶ When one gives a treatment for right
action and does not believe that right
action will be the result, he makes his
own treatment negative. Therefore, we
should spend much time in convincing
ourselves of the truth of our treatments.
Now this is not a power of will, but a
power of choice. We do not put the
power into the treatment, and we will
take out of the treatment only as much as
we believe is in it.

¶ If one doubts his ability to give an
effective treatment he should specifically

treat himself to remove this doubt. He should say something like this, but not necessarily these words: "I am convinced that this word has power, and I firmly believe in it. I trust it to produce the right results in my life," (or, in the life of the one for whom I am using my word).

¶ We should work, not with anxiety, but with expectancy, not by coercion, but with conviction, not through compulsion, but in a state of conscious recognition and receptivity. We do not have to drive or push but we must accept and believe. Then we should leave everything to the law, expecting a full and complete proof of our faith. We shall not be disappointed nor chagrined, for the law is our faithful servant.

¶ One should treat any given proposition until he proves his Principle, no matter how long it takes. We should treat until we get results, until there comes into our objective experience the actual outpouring of our subjective words.

¶ When working for someone else, speak the name of this person,—into Mind— then proceed with the treatment. Should someone come to you with the question, "Am I too old to find my rightful place?", what are you as a practitioner to reply? You explain that there is no recognition of age in the Truth, that everyone has his place in the Truth.

¶ A practitioner consciously removes the apparent obstruction and leaves the field open to a new influx of Spirit. He resolves things into thoughts, dissolves the negative appearance in the condition by recognizing only perfection. The practitioner must know and must state that there are no obstacles in the pathway of Truth. He must know that his word, being the activity of the Truth, removes all obstructions from the pathway of his patient, or the one for whom he is working.

¶ If the obstruction is the result of a "hang-over" from past years the practitioner must know that no past mistake can hinder or obstruct the flow of Divine Intelligence through God's idea,—which is perfect man, manifesting the attributes of God in freedom, happiness, activity and power, and that this Truth is now made manifest in his life.

¶ The patient should try to be receptive, not to the will of the practitioner, but to the purpose of the universe. That is, the patient should expect results and should be willing to give up anything and everything that would hinder the demonstration. If there is a stubbornness on the part of the patient the work of the practitioner will be more or less neutralized. Perfect belief is the beginning and the end of all good mental work.

¶ The mental attiude of the practitioner is one of denial toward every false condition that opposes the principle of Life as one of absolute perfection. God's world is perfect and this is the Principle we have to demonstrate.

¶A practitioner has no business with those who deny this Principle. The world as a whole does not believe in spiritual things, but this does not prevent the demonstration of Principle. Spiritual things must be spiritually discerned and when we are ready and willing spiritually to discern, we shall find a ready response from the invisible into the visible. For this reason children are often more easily reached than adults. Let the patient approach the Spirit with reverence and with receptivity and his problems will disappear as the mist before the sun. Let him approach in any other way and he will still be surrounded by the mists of his own unbelief. A practitioner may as well know these facts for they must be faced in his work. Everyone cannot be reached, because there are many who will not allow themselves to be helped. We did not make the law and it is certain that we cannot change its fundamental Principle, so it is useless to make the attempt.

¶ There are plenty of people who are ready and willing to be helped and to these we owe the obligation of our highest efforts. Let us do our work conscientiously and thoroughly and leave the results to that law which is perfect.

¶ A new light is coming into the world. We are on the borderland of a new experience. The veil between Spirit and matter is very thin. The invisible passes into visibility through our faith in it. A new science, a new religion, and a new philosophy are rapidly being developed. This is in line with the evolution of the great Presence and nothing can hinder its progress. It is useless as well as foolish to make any attempts to cover this Principle or to hold It as a vested right of any religion, sect or order. The Truth will out; the Spirit will make Itself known. Happy are we if we see these things which, from the foundation of the human race, have been longed for by all aspiring souls.

RELIGIOUS SCIENCE ¶ True thought deals directly with First Cause and Religious Science is the study of First Cause, Spirit, or the Truth, that Invisible Essence, that ultimate Stuff and Intelligence from which everything comes,—the Power back of creation,— The Thing Itself.

CPSIA information can be obtained at www.ICGtesting.com
Printed in the USA
BVOW080408160512

290346BV00003B/82/P